Fact Finders®

Life in the American Colonies

The Real Story about GOVERNMENT and POLITICS in Colonial America

by Kristine Carlson Asselin

Consultant:
Dr. Samuel B. Hoff
Professor of History
Delaware State University
Dover, Delaware

CAPSTONE PRESS
a capstone imprint

Fact Finders are published by Capstone Press,
1710 Roe Crest Drive, North Mankato, Minnesota 56003.
www.capstonepub.com

Library of Congress Cataloging-in-Publication Data
Asselin, Kristine Carlson.
The real story about government and politics in colonial America / by Kristine Carlson Asselin.
p. cm.—(Fact finders. Life in the American colonies)
Includes bibliographical references and index.
Summary: "Describes the government and political climate in colonial America"—Provided
by publisher.
ISBN 978-1-4296-6139-3 (library binding)
ISBN 978-1-4296-7219-1 (paperback)
1. United States—Politics and government—To 1775—Juvenile literature. I. Title. II. Series.
E188.A87 2012
973.2—dc22   2011004570

Editorial Credits

Jennifer Besel, editor; Ashlee Suker, designer; Wanda Winch, media researcher;
    Eric Manske, production specialist

Photo Credits

Alamy: North Wind Picture Archives, 8; The Bridgeman Art Library International: Peter Newark
American Pictures, 28; Capstone: 14; Getty Images Inc.: Time Life Pictures/Mansell, 11; The Granger
Collection, New York, 7, 15, 17, 25; Library of Congress: Prints and Photographs Division, 9, 19; NARA,
27, 29; National Parks Service: Harper's Ferry Center/Louis S. Glanzman, artist, cover; North Wind
Picture Archives, 13, 21, 22; Shutterstock: alexkar08, linen paper design element, F.C.G., 20, Irina
Tischenko, charred board design element, Labetskiy Alexandr Alexandrovich, floral background,
photocell, wood frame, Viachaslau Kraskouski, plank floor design

Printed in the United States of America in North Mankato, Minnesota.
082015   009140R

TABLE OF CONTENTS

Governing a New Land

When colonists first arrived in America, they had few plans for government. They had even fewer people who were prepared to lead. Without plans and good leaders, colonists had many disagreements. They couldn't agree on whether to farm or search for gold. They also didn't agree on how to treat the American Indians.

Millions of Indians lived in America when colonists arrived. The Indians had ancient traditions about who led the tribes. These traditions were different from those of the colonists. Misunderstandings led to fights between American Indians and colonists throughout the colonial period.

The colonial period lasted from 1607 to 1776. During this time, several countries tried to tame the wild land. France, Spain, Sweden, and the Netherlands all had settlements in America. But by 1754 the 13 British colonies were the only major European presence in America.

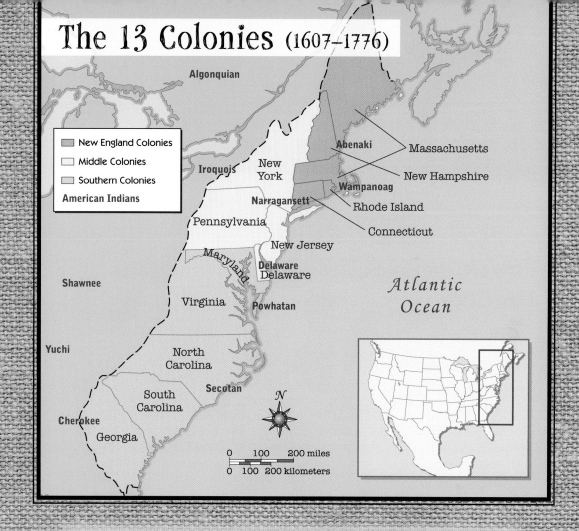

The 13 Colonies (1607–1776)

Algonquian

- New England Colonies
- Middle Colonies
- Southern Colonies
- American Indians

Iroquois

New York

Narragansett

Pennsylvania

Maryland

Delaware
Delaware

New Jersey

Shawnee

Virginia

Powhatan

Abenaki — Massachusetts

— New Hampshire

Wampanoag

Rhode Island

Connecticut

Atlantic Ocean

Yuchi

North Carolina

Secotan

South Carolina

Cherokee

Georgia

N

0   100   200 miles
0   100   200 kilometers

The British government didn't pay much attention to how the colonies were run. It was more interested in the money the colonies could make. So the colonists found their own ways to govern. Most colonies based their governments on the system in Great Britain.

Chapter 1

RULE in American Indian SOCIETIES

Long before colonists arrived, American Indian tribes had established different forms of government. These ruling systems served tribes in war and peace. Colonists did not always understand how tribal leadership worked.

The Iroquois (IHR-uh-kwoi) people lived in what is now New York. In Iroquois society, the sachem led only during war. During peacetime, Iroquois women were in charge. The women elected the sachem and decided when the community went to war. This idea was new for the colonists. The British colonists assumed men were the rulers. Speaking to the wrong Iroquois leader could be embarrassing or even deadly.

sachem—leader or chief

an illustration of an Iroquois Confederacy meeting

Iroquois Confederacy

According to legend, a prophet called the Peacemaker created a plan to end fighting among American Indian nations. The Peacemaker asked village leaders to come together to talk instead of using violence. Five nations joined together. They agreed to work together in war and peace. A sixth nation later joined the confederacy. The Iroquois Confederacy still exists today.

confederacy—a union of tribes with a common goal

THE POWHATAN CONFEDERACY

The Powhatan Indians lived near the colonial settlement of Jamestown, Virginia. A sachem named Powhatan ruled about 30 tribes and almost 15,000 people. This tribal organization came to be known as the Powhatan Confederacy. A council of advisors and village leaders helped Chief Powhatan make decisions.

Fast Fact

Pocahontas was a Powhatan Indian.

The Powhatans and colonists did not always agree. Here an artist shows Pocahontas asking Chief Powhatan to spare the life of colonial leader John Smith.

THE WAMPANOAG INDIANS

The Wampanoag (WAHM-puh-noh-ag) Indians lived in what became southeastern Massachusetts. The Wampanoag organized themselves into groups. Each group was led by a sachem.

The Pilgrims settled in Wampanoag territory in 1620. A sachem named Massasoit made a treaty with the Pilgrims. Both sides agreed to be peaceful and friendly. But the peace didn't last.

In fact, peace didn't last between American Indians and colonists anywhere in the colonies. As more colonists arrived, land became scarce. American Indians were pushed out of their homelands toward the west.

Massasoit and colonists agreeing on a peace treaty

9

Chapter 2

GOVERNMENT in the COLONIES

People couldn't just come to America and start a colony. They needed permission. For the 13 colonies, that permission came from Great Britain's king. The king decided who would be in charge of each colony.

Some colonies were founded by wealthy men. The king granted the men **charters**. Charters allowed the men to make all the decisions for their colonies.

For other colonies, the king chose one man as the proprietor. The proprietor chose the governor and ruled his colony like a king. In a royal colony, the king picked the governor.

In the late 1660s, the king tightened controls on the colonies. Eventually, all colonies except Rhode Island and Connecticut came under direct royal rule or were proprietary colonies.

Once the colonies were founded, Britain mostly ignored them. The royal government passed some laws for the colonies. But there were no punishments if the laws weren't followed.

William Penn, right, receiving the charter for Pennsylvania from King Charles II

As time passed, more and more people moved to America. It soon became important for each colony to have a formal system of government. Parliament gave the colonies permission to create laws and taxes. Colonies could also settle disagreements on their own.

Colonists based their governments on Great Britain's system. While each colony did things a bit differently, most had several things in common. Most colonies had a governor who answered to the king. They also had assemblies that created laws and councils to act as judges.

charter—a document that states the duties and rights of a group
Parliament—the governing body that makes the laws in Great Britain

GOVERNORS

For most colonies, the king or proprietor appointed a governor. The governor's role was to make decisions in place of the king or proprietor.

The governor had more power than anyone in the colony. He controlled a colony's army. He also decided when the assembly met. This group of elected leaders made laws for a colony. The governor could veto any laws the assembly created.

The governor could also decide when and how to hold elections for the assembly. Some governors set elections for inconvenient times and places. Governors made it difficult for people to vote so they could stay in control.

The governor's power was limited in one area. He could not control the colony's money. The assembly had this power. This limitation prevented governors from having too much control.

appoint—to choose someone for a job

veto—to stop a measure from becoming a law

an illustration of Governor Edmund Andros walking in the streets of Boston in 1689

A piece of paper money from Pennsylvania colony; 15 shillings could buy 1 pound (454 grams) of tea.

ASSEMBLY

Each town or county elected two citizens to the colony's assembly. Those elected were responsible for making laws that would govern everyone. But very few people were allowed to vote for assembly members. Slaves, American Indians, and women didn't get a vote. Most white males who did not own land couldn't vote either. For the most part, only white male landowners voted and were elected to the assembly.

The assembly made laws about how to tax colonists. They also made laws about trading and shipping. Laws accepted by the governor were sent to Great Britain for final approval. If the king approved, the law became official. The process could take up to six years.

an illustration of Virginia's House of Burgesses in 1619

To the frustration of many colonial governors, the assembly controlled a colony's money. Dividing power between the governor and assembly was an early form of checks and balances. Assemblies sometimes used this power to their advantage. An assembly could refuse to pay a governor's salary until he approved certain laws.

Fast Fact

Virginia created the first organized assembly in the colonies in 1619. It was called the House of Burgesses.

COUNCIL

The king appointed about 12 men to serve on the governor's council in each colony. The council, which was sometimes called the Senate, had three jobs. It enforced laws as the highest court in a colony. Council members gave advice to the governor. The council also served as a part of a colony's legislature. Laws passed by the assembly had to pass through the council to get to the governor. But council members and the governor had the same boss—the king. So this group usually took the governor's side in disagreements with the assembly.

Fast Fact

Council members were usually the wealthiest men in the colony. Most councilmen served for life, as long as they did not break the law.

legislature—a group of officials who have the power to make laws

a colonial leader speaking before the Virginia council

LOCAL GOVERNMENT

Towns had issues that only mattered to their residents. These issues might be about using a certain road or building a school. Town leaders kept order and made decisions that affected only their town.

Most town leaders were not elected. The governor appointed the sheriff, coroner, judges, and constables. The governor often filled these positions with family and friends.

Some towns had annual meetings to vote for selectmen. Selectmen, much like today's city council members, ran the local government. The selectmen appointed people to jobs to help run the town. Some of these jobs included keeper of the animal pound, weight and measurement sealer, and tax collector.

Fast Fact

Selectmen also appointed the fence viewer. This person made sure fences were in good shape.

an illustration of a
disorderly town meeting

coroner—a medical officer who investigates deaths
constable—a police officer

Chapter 3

CRIME and PUNISHMENT

People in colonial America were punished for things that might seem strange now. One man was found guilty of playing a bad practical joke. People who didn't go to church twice on Sunday were sometimes whipped. Telling lies and cheating were crimes too. Any of these crimes might land a person in the pillory or worse.

The pillory had holes for a criminal's hands and head. The person stood all day locked in the wooden structure. Townspeople threw rotten food at the lawbreaker's face.

Most criminals were also branded. A thief would get a "B" burned in the right hand. The "B" stood for burglary. Using fake money might earn someone an "R" for rogue. A branded hand made sure people always knew the person had committed a crime.

Slaves were treated like criminals. They were often branded with their masters' initials.

Very serious crimes, such as murder, resulted in hanging. Criminals could also be hanged if they stole grapes, hit their parents, or were caught spying.

Fast Fact

Hangings were entertainment for colonists. On the day of a hanging, people would bring a picnic and spend the afternoon.

Standing in the pillory was both hard on the body and embarrassing.

brand—to burn a mark onto the skin of a person

a woman on trial for witchcraft in 1692 in Salem, Massachusetts

TRIALS

A colonist accused of a crime had the right to a trial. At trial, colonists defended themselves. They could use a lawyer if they could afford one. It was more likely for a person to be found innocent in the colonies than in Britain. The colonies needed people who could work. So first offenses were often ignored.

One way to escape the worst punishments was to plead "benefit of clergy." If the person could say a Bible passage, he or she was spared the worst punishments. But a person could only use this escape plan once.

Salem Witch Trials

During the colonial period, many people believed in and feared witches. In 1692 two girls from Salem, Massachusetts, fell ill. They had seizures doctors didn't understand. People began to blame witches for the girls' problems. The fear of witches exploded. More than 150 people were put in jail for practicing witchcraft. No proof was presented at their trials. Many of the prisoners died in jail. At least 19 were hanged.

From the trial of accused witch Sarah Good on March 1, 1692

John Harthorn: Sarah Good what evil spirit have you familiarity with?

Sarah Good: None

Harthorn: Have you made no contract with the devil?

Good: No

Harthorn: Why do you hurt these children?

Good: I do not hurt them. I scorn it.

Harthorn: Who do you employ then to do it?

Good: No creature. But I am falsely accused.

Harthorn: Why did you go away muttering from Mr. Parris' house?

Good: I did not mutter, but I thanked him for what he gave my child.

[Spellings have been updated to be more readable.]

Sarah Good was hanged for witchcraft on July 19, 1692.

Chapter 4

GREAT BRITAIN
Gets Involved

Between 1689 and 1763, soldiers fought four wars in America. They were called the French and Indian Wars. Despite the name, the wars were really between France and Great Britain. Each side had support from American Indian tribes.

France and Britain were fighting for land in North America. Many people died in the battles. Eventually, Britain defeated France. France lost almost all its land in North America.

The wars cost Great Britain a lot of money. It was expensive to send troops to America. The colonies benefited from the successful ending of the war. Britain wanted them to pay their share of the cost.

King George III took the throne in 1760. Before his reign, Great Britain had never taxed the colonies. But to pay for the wars, the king and Parliament began taxing the colonies.

In 1765 Parliament passed the Stamp Act. This law added a tax to games such as cards and dice. It also taxed printed material and court papers. For the first time, a British tax directly affected the colonists.

The colonists were mad. They didn't get to vote for Parliament members. They didn't feel they should be taxed if they couldn't have a voice in the government. Mobs of angry colonists destroyed the homes of tax collectors. Citizens and British soldiers clashed in the streets. Violence left both American colonists and British soldiers dead.

Boston colonists attacked the lieutenant governor's home to protest the Stamp Act.

TOWNSHEND ACT

Parliament revoked the Stamp Act in 1766. But it continued to tax the colonies. In 1767 Parliament passed the Townshend Act. This law taxed glass, lead, paints, and tea. Colonial assemblies wrote long letters to Parliament. They expressed their frustration with the taxes. The colonists also began boycotting the products.

Parliament cancelled the Townshend Act in 1770, except for the tea tax. In a sneaky move, Parliament worked with the tea distributor to lower the price of tea. Parliament leaders thought colonists would pay the lower price even though it still included the tax. They were wrong.

revoked—to take away or cancel

boycott—to refuse to buy a product to protest something believed to be wrong

Virginia leader Patrick Henry, center, speaking to the assembly against the Townshend Act.

"In England there can be no taxation without representation, and no representation without election; but it is undeniable that the representatives of Great-Britain are not elected by nor for the Americans, and therefore cannot represent them ..."

—Reverend John Zubly in a 1769 pamphlet

THE BOSTON TEA PARTY

Most colonists didn't feel Parliament had a right to tax them. To prove their point, colonists in New York and Philadelphia turned away ships carrying tea. But in Boston, the governor let the ships dock. A group called the Sons of Liberty took extreme action.

Two hundred men stormed the ships. They threw crates of tea into the ocean. They destroyed 45 tons (41 metric tons) of tea.

The king and Parliament were furious. They closed the Port of Boston. Then they took all positions in the assembly away from local citizens. The positions were given to British supporters. Parliament also sent British troops into the city. Boston no longer had any freedom.

Some members of the Sons of Liberty dressed as American Indians to disguise themselves as they destroyed the tea.

INDEPENDENCE

The rest of the colonies feared they could be treated like Boston. From September 5 to October 26, 1774, colonial leaders gathered at the First Continental Congress. They explored how colonial government could work with Britain's government.

Within a year, shots were fired in Lexington, Massachusetts. The Second Continental Congress declared war with Great Britain. Leaders decided the colonies needed an independent government. The colonies would no longer be British properties but 13 united states.

colonial leaders signing the Declaration of Independence

GLOSSARY

appoint (uh-POINT)—to choose someone for a job

boycott (BOY-kot)—to refuse to buy or use a product or service to protest something believed to be wrong or unfair

brand (BRAND)—to burn a mark onto the skin of a person or animal

charter (CHAR-tuhr)—a formal document that states the duties and rights of a group of people

confederacy (kuhn-FED-ur-uh-see)—a union of tribes, states, towns, or people with a common goal

constable (KON-stuh-buhl)—a police officer in Great Britain and the British colonies

coroner (KOR-uh-nur)—a medical officer who investigates deaths

legislature (LEJ-iss-lay-chur)—a group of officials who have the power to make or change laws

Parliament (PAR-luh-muhnt)—the governing body that makes the laws in Great Britain

revoke (ri-VOKE)—to take away or cancel

sachem (SAY-chuhm)—leader or chief

veto (VEE-toh)—to stop a measure from becoming a law

READ MORE

Kelly, Martin, and Melissa Kelly. *Government.* Colonial Life. Armonk, N.Y.: M.E. Sharpe, 2008.

Raum, Elizabeth. *The Dreadful, Smelly Colonies: The Disgusting Details about Life During Colonial America.* Disgusting History. Mankato, Minn.: Capstone Press, 2010.

Strum, Richard M. *Causes of the American Revolution.* Road to War. Stockton, N.J.: OTTN Pub., 2006.

INTERNET SITES

FactHound offers a safe, fun way to find Internet sites related to this book. All of the sites on FactHound have been researched by our staff.

Here's all you do:

Visit *www.facthound.com*

Type in this code: 9781429661393

Check out projects, games and lots more at
www.capstonekids.com

31

INDEX

PRIMARY SOURCE BIBLIOGRAPHY

Page 23—taken from the transcript of the examination of Sarah Good on March 1, 1692, written by Ezekiell Chevers, as printed by the University of Missouri-Kansas City School of Law Salem Witchcraft Trials project Web site
Page 27—taken from Reverend John Zubly's 1769 pamphlet titled *An Humble Enquiry into the Nature of the Dependency of the American Colonies upon the Parliament of Great-Britain, and the Right of Parliament to Lay Taxes on the Said Colonies*